THE ILLUSTRATED HARVARD

THE ILLUSTRATED HARVARD

Harvard University in Wood Engravings and Words

by MICHAEL McCURDY

The Globe Pequot Press

Chester, Connecticut 06412

For Deborah

Text and illustrations © 1986 by Michael McCurdy

❋ ❋ ❋

Library of Congress Cataloging-in-Publication Data

McCurdy, Michael.

The illustrated Harvard.

1. McCurdy, Michael.   2. Harvard University in art.

3. Harvard University—Buildings. I. Title.

NE1112.M33A4   1986   378.744'4   86–316

ISBN 0-87106-896-6

First Edition/First Printing

For three-and-a-half centuries, Harvard, the first (and for more than fifty years, only) institution of higher learning in North America, has grown mainly according to its needs and opportunities. It has had no master planners along the lines of Peter the Great, Thomas Jefferson, or Baron Georges Haussmann. The earliest college buildings—wooden structures accommodating the president, a handful of students, and the first printing press in British North America—stood on two-and-one-third acres of allotted land. Today, in Cambridge alone, Harvard fills and, in its vertical expansion, even overfills an area one hundred times larger than that. It has reached north to the Law School and Radcliffe, south to the river houses, and across the Charles to Soldier's Field, the Business School, and the medical complex. Among the two dozen or so colleges and universities in the Boston area, only Harvard's faculty and students often refer, perhaps pardonably, to their school not by name but as "here."

To the extent that it has a campus in the usual sense of the word, Harvard's is the entire Harvard Square section of Cambridge. In turn, the university, one of Cambridge's largest industries, has become part of the city's public and psychic space. There may be tensions between the two communities, but, like an old married couple, they can't live without each other. They've managed to stand more or less side by side through the American Revolution—when Washington's Continental Army billeted in the Yard and bivouacked on the Common—the "trashing" of Harvard Square in 1970 during the height of the anti–Vietnam War protest, and debates over recombinant DNA research and the location of the Kennedy Library.

Few other places on this continent display such a dazzle of contrasting architectures (by Colonial builders, antiquarians, and academic journeymen; by Bulfinch and Richardson; by McKim, Mead and White; by Gropius; by Le Corbusier; and by James Stirling) and contrasting idioms: Georgian and neo-Georgian, Greek Revival, Federal, Romanesque, Colonial and Colonial Revival, Collegiate neo-Gothic, Gold Coast Whimsical, Beaux Arts, W.P.A. Modern, International Style, and just plain indescribable. The New Brutalism, an architecture of poured concrete represented by Sert's Holyoke Center and Undergraduate Science Center, was no newcomer to Cambridge, having been anticipated at the turn of the century by Harvard Stadium. A relic of the golden age of Ivy League football and, to go even farther back in time, an evocation of Roman circuses and Greek amphitheaters, the stadium was nonetheless forward-looking and boldly experimental.

Memorial Hall, a theater, a commons (as originally intended), and a somber transept faced with marble tablets listing Harvard's Civil War dead, continues to dominate the university complex. A cathedral mated with a railroad terminal, polychrome Victorian Gothic Memorial Hall has passed through cycles of execration as well as praise to remain Harvard's one heroic building, a stronger presence than the imperial bulk of Widener Library. At the very least, the strength of Memorial Hall resides in the fact that, like the Matterhorn or the Statue of Liberty, it is so undeniably *there* that one can't imagine the landscape without it.

A few yards away stands the School of Design's Gund Hall, a thoroughly contemporary structure that in its shape and siting nevertheless pays tribute to its eclectic neighbor. Less accommodating is Minoru Yamasaki's William James Hall. This fifteen-story monolith, the tallest of Harvard's Cambridge buildings (it is topped with a red warning light for passing aircraft), looks like a refrigerator, generates arctic gusts that roar down its face into Kirkland Street, and has little to do with the adjacent Busch–Reisinger Museum, a souvenir of the Holy Roman

Empire. Equally indifferent to its surroundings, two blocks to the south, Le Corbusier's Carpenter Center for the Visual Arts squats between two buildings of entirely alien style and scale and has reminded some visitors of two grand pianos making love on a very small bed. Still, it is Le Corbusier's only building in the United States and to some extent makes up for the omission of Frank Lloyd Wright from Harvard's distinguished roster of architects.

Scattered through the mélange of Harvard construction are extraordinary vestiges and surprises: Flemish gables and Jacobean ornamentation; cartouches that blazon the pediments of Holden Chapel like a flourish of baroque trumpets; the visionary skyline of domes, bell towers, and facades rising over the banks of the Charles. One could call all this a vast outdoor museum if it were not that even the oddest buildings, the most glaring anachronisms in style and design, are in some sort of working order, either through maintenance or recycling.

Michael McCurdy's luminous, deceptively straightforward wood engravings offer a convenient walking tour of bricks-and-mortar Harvard. Their stark black-and-whiteness suggests the well-known agonizings of the New England conscience as well as the values locally associated with simplicity and self-reliance. These pictures convey a haunted, lonely atmosphere. Except for a few isolated pairs of human figures for scale, McCurdy's vistas are mostly empty of people. He's concerned with stability, not the flux of Harvard Square and its pageant of tourists, shoppers, peddlers, street performers, and consumers of ice cream. This section of Cambridge is now one of the eastern seaboard's obligatory sights. Perhaps something precious has been lost in the process of growth and sophistication: village and collegiate intimacy along with such homely fixtures as cafeterias, lunch counters, and a Woolworth's. But the brick sidewalks, lilacs, magnolias, and residential streets remain, along with a student population that renews itself each year like the seasons.

THE ILLUSTRATED HARVARD

Lehman Hall and Straus Hall

Facing Harvard Square, Lehman Hall (now part of Dudley House) on the right and Straus Hall on the left greet all visitors who start their tour of Harvard University from the Square. Lehman, built in 1925, was given by Arthur Lehman and originally housed the University's business office. It now serves as a nonresident student facility. Straus Hall, added a year later, was a gift of the Straus brothers, students in the 1890s, in honor of their parents, who had perished with the *Titanic* in 1912.

Matthews Hall and Grays Hall

Entering the gate shown in the previous engraving, we find ourselves in Harvard Yard and in front of Matthews Hall. At the time it was built in 1871, Matthews was called the finest college dormitory in America. This example of architectural bravado was the gift of Nathan Matthews, a Boston merchant whose son was a Harvard student at the time. The elder Matthews stipulated that half of the net income from the dormitory be used to aid needy and deserving students. Matthews Hall and three other dormitories of that time were blessed with indoor plumbing in the basement, thus eliminating the need for the row of outhouses (fondly called University Minor) that had graced the end of University Hall nearby. The dormitory called Grays Hall, to the left, was built earlier, in 1863, and is on the site of the "Old College," which was the very first Harvard building. Grays Hall was the first dormitory to be equipped with cold running water.

Massachusetts Hall

This is the Yard's earliest existing building, completed in 1720. It served as a barracks for Continental troops from 1775 to 1776, when Harvard was moved to the relative safety of Concord during those opening years of the Revolutionary War. It was primarily a dormitory until 1871, and although it is now the location of the office of the president, some student rooms still command views from the top floor. The Unitarian Church in the background, seen across Massachusetts Avenue, was built in 1833 and was used by Harvard College for commencement exercises for forty years afterward.

Harvard Hall and Lionel Hall

The present Harvard Hall stands on the site of the first building to bear that name, which was begun in the early 1670s and was the second building constructed for the College. The first Harvard Hall burned to the ground in 1764, and some 5,000 volumes in the College library were destroyed. Rebuilt between the years 1764 and 1766, Harvard Hall was altered in 1842 and was enlarged in 1870 to its present design. Today it is used primarily for classrooms. Lionel Hall, a dormitory to the left, appears considerably older than it is. It was actually built in 1925 in memory of Lionel de Jersey Harvard, Class of 1915, who was killed in France on March 30, 1918.

Hollis Hall, Holden Chapel, and Stoughton Hall

Hollis Hall, the dormitory shown on the left, served in 1775 as a barracks for Continental troops. It had been built thirteen years earlier, in 1762, to honor Thomas Hollis of London, a merchant who along with other members of his family had helped finance the College since the year 1719. Hollis Hall was a dormitory for both Ralph Waldo Emerson and Henry David Thoreau. Between Hollis Hall and Stoughton Hall is Holden Chapel, built in 1742 and one of the oldest buildings on campus. Not only was Holden the College's first chapel, but it served as Harvard's first medical school as well. It currently houses the Harvard–Radcliffe Choral Society. Stoughton Hall, nearly an exact copy of Hollis, was built in 1805 and was named for William Stoughton, who had given an earlier Stoughton Hall. The current dormitory was built with the assistance of funds from a state-run lottery.

Holworthy Hall and Thayer Hall

The barracks-like Holworthy Hall, shown on the left, was completed in 1812 with the proceeds of the state lottery. The dormitory was named in honor of Sir Matthew Holworthy, Harvard's principal benefactor in the seventeenth century, who had given £1,000 to the College in 1681. Holworthy Hall boasted the first use of gas lighting on the campus, installed in recitation rooms in 1855. Thayer Hall, on the right, was the first of the large Harvard dormitories and was built in 1869 to house the growing number of students who could not afford the rising costs of rooms outside the College. Funds came from Nathaniel Thayer, a Harvard graduate and Boston businessman. The building was constructed to honor the donor's father as well as his brother John Eliot Thayer, who established the Thayer Scholarships.

Weld Hall and University Hall

A gift of William Weld, a Boston financier, in memory of his brother Stephen Minot Weld, Weld Hall was constructed in 1870 and was designed by Ware and Van Brunt, the same architects whose Memorial Hall was under construction at the time. Weld Hall is now a dormitory for first-year students. A portion of University Hall is also shown in this view from the steps of Widener Library. Completed in 1815 and designed by the renowned architect Charles Bulfinch, University Hall today houses administrative offices. The famous statue of John Harvard by Daniel Chester French stands in front of the Hall on the opposite side. The model for the statue was Sherman Hoar, a Harvard student during the 1880s.

Widener Library

One of the largest libraries in the United States, Widener has well over three million books and about ten miles of stacks. This enormous edifice was constructed between 1913 and 1915 with funds donated by the mother of Harry Elkins Widener. Her son was graduated from Harvard in 1907 and went down with the *Titanic* five years later.

Memorial Church

Facing Widener Library, Memorial Church was erected in 1931 primarily to honor the Harvard men who had died in World War I. It also serves as a memorial for all Harvard students and alumni who lost their lives in other wars. Memorial Church was built on the site of Appleton Chapel, which had been erected in 1856. Religious services are held weekly, and graduating students receive their degrees in front of the church.

Canaday Hall, Memorial Hall, and Robinson Hall

As we reach the northern edge of Harvard Yard, we see on the left a portion of the newest Yard dormitory, Canaday Hall, which was constructed with funds donated by Ward Murphy Canaday, who was graduated from Harvard in 1907. Memorial Hall can be seen across busy Cambridge Street, somewhat isolated in its grandeur. To the right is Robinson Hall, designed by McKim, Mead and White and completed in 1904 in memory of Nelson Robinson Jr., who was to have been graduated in 1900 but had died in his junior year. Because of Robinson's profound interest in landscape architecture, the country's very first classes in this developing field were held in this building. Robinson Hall, once the home of the Graduate School of Design, now provides space for the Department of History.

Memorial Hall

Henry James referred to Memorial Hall as "the great bristling brick Valhalla." Completed in July 1878, this monumental example of high Victorian excess, 305 feet long, honors the 136 Harvard men who died fighting for the Union during the Great Rebellion. Originally it was Harvard's dining hall, a gathering ground for alumni, and a place for meetings and entertainment. It lost its topmost steeple during a 1956 fire. Memorial Hall contains Sanders Theatre, which seats 1,200 and was built with a bequest from Charles Sanders, who had been graduated from Harvard in 1802.

Busch-Reisinger Museum

This deliberately eclectic building, seen in this view from the apse of Memorial Hall, was designed by a Dresden architect to reflect the various periods of central and northern European art represented in the Museum. The building and some early collections were the gifts of Adolphus Busch, a German–American brewer, and his son-in-law Hugo Reisinger. Construction was begun in 1914, but because World War I delayed the building's completion, it did not open until 1921.

Harvard Law School

Shown here is a portion of Austin Hall, a gift of the prominent merchant Edward
Austin. Designed by H. H. Richardson and built between 1881 and 1883, it was
the only building of the Law School until 1907. Prominently engraved near the
top of Austin Hall is an inscription that runs almost its entire length: AND THOU
SHALT TEACH THEM ORDINANCES AND LAWS AND SHALT SHEW THEM THE WAY
WHEREIN THEY MUST WALK AND THE WORK THEY MUST DO. On the evening of
June 16, 1775, 1,200 Continental soldiers assembled on this site under the command of Colonel William Prescott, who stopped for prayers before marching on
to the battle of Bunker Hill.

Radcliffe Yard

From the Law School it's an easy walk across Cambridge Common to Radcliffe Yard, the center for the women's college. The Elizabeth Cary Agassiz House, shown on the left, was built in 1904 and currently houses offices for the arts and student organizations as well as the Agassiz Theatre. The building was named for Radcliffe College's first president, who was the wife of the Harvard naturalist Louis Agassiz. The Hemenway Gymnasium, at the right, was built in 1898 and provides space for a dance program and a social services data center for women.

Wadsworth House

Returning to our starting point, we find this handsome remnant of Cambridge's colonial era at the edge of Harvard Yard, facing Massachusetts Avenue. Wadsworth House was the home of nine Harvard presidents, from Benjamin Wadsworth, who was in office at the time it was built, to Edward Everett, who served from 1846 to 1849. Built in 1726, it is the second-oldest Harvard building still in existence, and it has been well used over the years as (among others things) a boarding house, a dormitory, and the office of the College printer. It served as the lodgings for General Washington throughout July 1775. Harvard's Alumni Association is now located here. The newer addition, also called Wadsworth, was built in 1810 but was moved to its present location in 1871. Portions of Grays Hall and Widener Library are also shown.

Wigglesworth Hall

This freshman dormitory, constructed in 1930, is made up of two buildings that serve to wall off the Yard from noisy Massachusetts Avenue. The tunnel that cuts directly through one of the buildings is shown here and is one of several entrances to the Yard that are always open. Wigglesworth Hall was named in honor of a long line of Wigglesworths who had strong connections with the College, beginning with Michael Wigglesworth, a poet, pastor, and tutor who was graduated in 1651. The present Hall stands on the site of a house owned by the Wigglesworth family in the early 1700s.

Plympton Street

Connecting Mount Auburn Street with Massachusetts Avenue, Plympton Street is one of the more interesting side streets in the area. The Grolier Book Shop—a veritable mecca for poetry lovers since 1927—is flanked by the Harvard Bookstore and the 1916 *Harvard Crimson* building. Next comes a portion of the rambling Adams House dormitory complex, named after President John Adams, who was graduated from Harvard in 1755. This part of Adams House was constructed in 1931.

The Lampoon *Building*

The *Harvard Lampoon* began in 1876 when a note was surreptitiously passed in class proposing a humor magazine based on England's *Punch*. Its building, completed in 1910, was constructed of "bench brick"—brick that is burned and somewhat irregular—and a variety of roofing tiles from several countries. Its outrageous design is a joke in brick and mortar.

Lowell House

Named for A. Lawrence Lowell, a president of Harvard, this dormitory was built during his administration in 1930. In its belfry is a set of Russian bells that originally hung in a monastery near Moscow. They were purchased from the Soviet government by Charles Crane, the plumbing manufacturer, who presented them to Harvard in 1931. The bells have an eastern musical scale that make them difficult for westerners to play well.

Eliot House and Smith Halls

Eliot House, built in 1931, was named for the great educator and long-time Harvard president Charles Eliot, who was largely responsible for turning Harvard from a college into a university of international importance. This impressive example of Harvard's river houses stands next to Smith Halls, a part of Kirkland House, constructed in 1914. Some "houses" are actually large undergraduate dormitory complexes made up of "halls" that bear different names from those of their houses.

Harvard Business School

Seen from the Weld Boathouse in Cambridge, the Business School looms on the Boston side of the Charles River. These buildings were constructed in the 1920s, after the august firm of McKim, Mead and White (which had designed Robinson Hall) won a competition for the design. The Business School campus was designed around the Baker Library, shown in the center of this engraving. In its early days, the Business School held its classes on the top floor of Widener Library.

Weld Boathouse

As we walk across the General Nathaniel Anderson Bridge (commonly called the Larz Anderson Bridge) over the Charles River, a backward glance gives us a view of the Weld Boathouse, completed in 1907. Although thoroughly identified with Harvard, the Weld Boathouse is owned not by Harvard but by the Weld Trustees. It was built with a bequest of George Weld, Class of 1860, and serves as one of two Harvard boathouses. The interior is taken up mostly by the sculls and shells that glide up and down the Charles.

Dunster House

Looking east from the Anderson Bridge, we see Dunster House rising above the trees and the Charles River. Completed in 1932, the dormitory was named for the first president of Harvard, Henry Dunster, who held the position from 1640 to 1654. The John W. Weeks Bridge, shown in this scene, although no longer Harvard property, was designed by McKim, Mead and White and built in 1927. It bears the name of the late U.S. Senator and Secretary of War during the Harding administration.

Harvard Stadium

Harvard Stadium was one of the earliest examples of the large-scale use of reinforced concrete. It was erected between 1901 and 1903 and completed just in time for the Harvard–Yale game of that year. The stadium, which has a seating capacity of 22,000, was paid for largely by the twenty-fifth-reunion gift of the Class of 1879. Although its ivy is now gone, Harvard Stadium became known as one of the handsomest college stadiums in the country by virtue of its graceful arches and ivy-covered walls. The colonnade atop the stadium was added in 1910.

Harvard Medical School

Far removed from Harvard Yard and the sprawling contemporary campus found in Cambridge, Harvard Medical School is located in Boston's Fenway district. The School was moved from Cambridge to Boston because it had to be in close proximity to the many prominent hospitals in that city. The School was founded in 1782, with its first lectures being held in Harvard Hall and Holden Chapel. It has had a number of Boston addresses ever since. In 1903 construction on the present site was begun under the direction of President Eliot. Much later, in 1964, the Francis Countway Library was added; it is shown here between the building on the right, the administration building, and the one at the left, which was built to house laboratories. Today Harvard Medical School is virtually surrounded by hospitals and other medical facilities.

About the Artist

Michael McCurdy, a well-known illustrator and book designer, also prints and publishes first-edition poetry, fiction, and translations under the distinguished Penmaen Press imprint.

His beautifully designed and produced volumes have won numerous awards both here and abroad.

Writing on the technique of wood engraving, McCurdy notes: "[It] is an honest medium. It's straightforward and there is no room for error. . . . A cut is made, and it stays."

A graduate of Boston's School of the Museum of Fine Arts and Tufts University, McCurdy works from a studio on his property in Great Barrington, Massachusetts.

A Note on These Engravings

Thomas Carlisle called it "the fine art of scratch." And you could say that about wood engraving. Images are often scratched rather than deeply cut into the one-inch-high endgrain woodblocks. What is cut away from the obdurate wood are areas that appear white in the final print. Tools of various shapes release the lighter images from the block's inked and somber surface, and one slip of the burin may mean many hours' work wasted.

For me, the most difficult part of the task was not the time-consuming engraving of the wood, with my head bent low over a block and my nose sometimes pressing directly onto the magnifying glass that served as my window on the scene. My greatest challenge lay in the preparation of the drawings, the result of many trips to Harvard University with sketchpad and camera. And it was difficult to decide, out of all the brick, mortar, and glass that make up the physical Harvard, just what I should include and what had to be left out. Selecting the most effective composition was often trying when I repeatedly found myself at ground level looking up, distracted by pedestrians, street signs, and rushing motor vehicles.

Harvard is, of course, too large and diverse to be fully captured in a series of woodblocks from which images in printer's ink are to be pulled. This collection of wood engravings can be thought of as a walking tour of some of Harvard's many libraries, schools, halls, and museums as well as a sampling of its architectural history of the past 350 years.

Michael McCurdy
Great Barrington, Massachusetts